Just some thoughts from one Black woman.

Thoughts to ponder as race relations still have a long road to travel.

TABLE OF CONTENTS

When many hear the term racism, they believe it is merely discrimination, a slur, or simply hating someone because of the color of their skin. More than 60 years ago – The Civil Rights Movement, 1954-1968, sent direct, in your face racism underground. It became illegal and less socially acceptable to slur or discriminate against someone openly. With overt racism being banished to a sound-proof corner of the mind, America deemed racism over and there was to be nothing more done about it. "We will not openly dismiss you." In public, America's actions and statements were "you're great", but in private, America would set aside pretenses and blame Black Americans for their own ongoing struggles. "Hey, we did our part, we banned public racism, and any failures from this point on are on you, your own moral failure."

After many setbacks and slow starts, many stated that Blacks just had a lot of problems within their culture and within their value system. America attributed the failings of Black Americans on Black Americans. That the problems of Blacks stemmed from their own making, their violence and laziness. These were sentiments that reverberated across the country. Many did not see this as racism, just facts. "We are not doing anything to them, they are doing it to themselves." The message being echoed was "to be Black, was to be inferior."   But these were not facts, they were just racism cloaked in disdain, a way for America to disguise their thoughts that Black people were unworthy. It needs to be understood that racism is not just overt, individuals prancing around in white hoods or burning crosses; racism is a system of discrimination – it is subtle injustice that has been established and upheld by societal institutions.

Figure 1 Abraham Lincoln signed the document of freedom, but Black America would not be truly free.

The signing of the document, the Emancipation Proclamation, declared "that all persons held as slaves are, and henceforward shall be free", what did this really mean for Black Americans?   It seemed promising initially but then as time went on the system just seemed designed to keep Blacks in a permanent state of second-class status. It seemed to be a system steeped with stereotyping. Yes, the Jim Crow Laws were changed, but they were just replaced with what was viewed better on paper. The laws still bore the signs of racism. The new laws just made it harder for those looking closely to see the true reality. Whites began with a huge advantage and Blacks were left in a fight for equal footing. The obstacles just kept mounting and no matter how hard they tried or how determined they were, Black Americans could not catch up. The signing of the document that meant freedom may have been well intentioned but Black Americans would need more than pen to paper to capitalize on that freedom.

Looking back, how were Black Americans ultimately relegated to a lower class of citizenry? How did they seemingly get to a permanent state of second class? Well, it began where many things in this country began – with money. For roughly 30 years (about 1934 to 1962) the government would back billions of dollars for home loans, but guess what? Yes, you guessed it, the loans were only available to Whites. And of course, this began a domino effect. This forced Blacks into less prominent areas and eventually created what would be called "ghettos" and thus the birth of segregated America. This wealth disparity made it impossible to invest in the future of Black neighborhoods, and it made it impossible for Black Americans to inherit property and wealth leaving them far behind their White counterparts.

Figure 2 It seemed there would be no pot of gold at the end of this rainbow.

But the divide did not stop there, education and fair waged jobs would be afforded to White Americans, but again Black Americans were short – changed. Because they could not get loans to live in better neighborhoods, not owning any property, Blacks paid no property taxes. The payment of property taxes fund schools. So, what did this translate to? Those who lived in nice houses paid property taxes and they in turn received a better education and a better education meant more opportunities, more resources, more connections, more jobs, and in turn more money.

The path for Black Americans continued to be lined with obstacles. A lack of education and educational opportunities meant Blacks were relegated to low-waged jobs and manual labor. Now there is absolutely nothing wrong with manual labor, the country was built on manual labor, but without the education aspect, Blacks, it seemed, would not stop straddling hurdles that were destined to keep them behind Whites in wealth, education, and job advancement. The takeaway here is that Black Americans started their freedom and journey to achieving the American dream decades behind White Americans. So, the question should have been, what will America do to help them catch up?

Figure 3 Would hope come?

Moving into present day, Americans must ask one question, does it seem that we are still in a bygone era? It is now the 21st century and some elements of American society have not released their hold on a time when one group made it their mission to dominate or reign superior over another. Slavery was prohibited in 1865. In 1866 Congress passed the Civil Rights Act, conferring citizenship on Black Americans, granting them equal rights to whites. In 1870 Black American males were given the right to vote. In 1881 states passed "Jim Crow", separate but equal, segregation laws. With these laws, of course, Black Americans were not allowed *equal* access to public facilities.

It was in 1954 that the case of Brown vs Board of Education ruled that segregation was unconstitutional. In 1955, the defiant act of Rosa Parks gave momentum to the Civil Rights Movement. In 1964 The Civil Rights Act was signed, prohibiting discrimination of all kinds. Enter the 21st century, in 2008, America elected its first Black President.

There were subtle signs of inequality, but some events of the 21st century made it seem as if no progress at all had been made as protesters would take to the streets again to fight for the right just to live with no fear of death by those sworn to protect or hated them simply because of the color of their skin. Why is it so hard for America to see people of color as equal?

Figure 4 A dream pledged; a dream deferred.

"True peace is not merely the absence of tension: it is the presence of Justice," Martin Luther King, Jr., this was his response in 1955, when he was accused of disturbing the peace during the Montgomery Bus Boycott in Alabama.

Within the 21st century there have been incidences that put the inequalities of people of color on full display. The injustices did not suddenly surface, there were subtle, covert injustices happening every day.   Are Americans ready to live in a world where injustice for people of color is tolerated, accepted, and thrust back into an era of yesteryear? Are Americans ready to return to the days when people of color are openly and publicly disrespected despite their accomplishments (Republican Arizona Governor, Jan Brewer wagging her finger in the President's face in 2012, President Barack Obama, the first Black president); when people of color are publicly degraded (when Republican Representative Joe Wilson of South Carolina yelled "You Lie!" during President Obama's address to Congress September 2009); when people of color are gassed because they dare to be upset at their treatment (riots in Ferguson, Missouri, 2014)?

People of color have struggled as far back as many can remember. It seemed that every day would begin and end with some mental or physical battle. Every day Blacks would awake believing and hoping that things would get better. And for a while it seemed things did, there was the election of a man of color to the most powerful position in the country. This was a promising day. But soon after Blacks were forced back to reality. They were forced to realize that not much had changed at all since the Civil Rights movement. With the election of President Obama, overt racism was back with a vengeance thus revealing a momentum deception.

Figure 5 A bridge too far? America continues to struggle with equality, struggling to get over the bridge, the hurdle.

Black Americans wanted to believe there was forward motion and the language of policies and legislation allowed us to maintain that belief. We needed to feel that things were getting better, and the law's rhetoric made it unacceptable to publicly voice or openly display disdain for people of color. And because society was forced to suppress its true feelings, these feelings were forced to lie dormant for decades. But the culture that is racism reared its ugly head again and reality came to the forefront in 2008 when Barack Obama assumed his position to the highest post in the land. At that point, for eight years, Black Americans, were forced to face a reality – that we were not accepted as equal, no matter our status or position.

Figure 6 A glimmer of hope, but it came with a price.

When individuals can find fault in any and every action of a President who is highly accomplished simply because of the color of his skin, the writing is on the wall. With a president of color, conversations seemed to always steer in the vicinity of origin, creed, and nationality – the rights that were not to be questioned anymore because they were supposed to be bestowed on all Americans. People of color, quickly discovered that after decades of believing they were truly accepted, found they were not really accepted at all, but merely tolerated.

People of color, it must be faced, are not considered equal. This became abundantly clear with every injustice that took place during the eight years of President Obama's tenure and beyond. It seemed people of color were tolerated, maybe, but the moment they attempted to break barriers, there was someone there to remind them that they were inferior, that they were only allowed to advance so far and then they were put back in their place. Yes, there have been great advancements made by people of color and many can head to coveted safe zones where they are allowed to escape reality, but the cap cannot be put back on this bottle, Blacks cannot un-endure what they have endured in the past decades. They can no longer wear the blinders and pretend that racism does not exist just because they may be far removed from it – it exists, although in many cases, subtle. *"Shallow understanding from people of good will is more frustrating than absolute misunderstanding from people of ill will. Lukewarm acceptance is much more bewildering than outright rejection,"* Martin Luther King, Jr. said this about white moderates and opposition within the Black community.

Figure 7 Barbara Jordan, the first Black American elected to the Texas Senate and the first Black American woman elected to the US House of Representatives. Acceptance, probably not?

But people of color, as much as some would hate to admit, are equal, they are just as good as anyone else. Many times, they are better because we have overcome adversity and still, they rise. They are educated, they are accomplished, they are survivors, they are doers, and they are CAN-doers; because with a lifetime of struggle in their past, they still rise. For people of color, struggle is no stranger. People of color, do not give those who wish to stifle you the ammunition they need to show you in a bad light. Push forward with your minds and intellect – you are better than those who continue to hold to the stance that you are inferior. Beat the nay-sayers with kindness, with resilience, and with staying power.

Figure 8 The crew of the Space Shuttle Columbia. The crew was lost during re-entry on February 1, 2003. The color of America.

I, a Black American, am, however, sometimes left saddened, a little dismayed, and a bit hopeless that the American society has revealed the truth of what it thinks of people of color. Why, in what is supposed to be the greatest country, can the people not let go of an antiquated thought process? Why is making people of color feel inferior so important? What do you get out of it? Try answering these questions and then maybe, as a society, we can get past the need to make others feel less-than.

And as Americans ponder why it is so important for this society to hold on to an outdated reality, I, myself, must come to grips with my own naivety, how I was fooled by the grand pretense. I was so trusting and believing. I believed that progress had been made, that if people of color, individually failed it was because they did not try hard enough – because after all no one can stop another's success – this is America and ALL have freedoms and rights. But I was forced to open my eyes to the reality that is the society in which I have grown up and believed to be a fair and just society, that it is not always that fair.

The grand pretense would be put front and center when America would later allow someone with clear disdain for people of color to hold the most powerful position in the country. America would let people of color know exactly how they felt about them when they would allow someone to ascend to the highest position in the land who would completely sever any hope of equality in the nation and who would destroy all hopes of America ever truly being a "united" society. This would become a clear indicator that people of color were not seen as equal. It would be this action that would confirm the belief of half of America, that they did not believe that people of color were equal.

Figure 9 The grand pretense. Black Americans were still not destined to see clear skies and white sands.

So, I was left asking myself, why did I blindly or willingly accept that equality was mine? Did I simply want to believe so badly that I was equal that all the warning signs that might have been revealed escaped me or were simply ignored? Was it because acknowledging those signs would mean that my grandparents, my parents, and even my own efforts were futile, people of color, were never going to be given a fair and equal chance to achieve all that was achievable?

I cannot answer why it took me so long to wake up – maybe it was a hope that I was wrong in believing that three generations of my family having protected a country and an illusion of an inalienable right that we would never have, kept me from waking up. That I had defended a country that does not care about me because of the color of my skin; that people of color are merely a tolerance that the society must put up with because after all there needs to be someone on the bottom so that the elitist can reign supreme.

Figure 10 Inalienable right, no surrender.

How dare I believe that we are all equal? How dare my parents and grandparents tell me that I live in a free society, and I can be anything I choose? Who is to blame for this misrepresentation to me and all people of color? Who told us we could have the American dream? No one ever told me that there would be limitations on the dream.

I believe I can state with certainty that this nation, our society, has revealed its true colors in the last few decades. The disguise of carefully worded policies and laws that were designed to give us all equal and shared rights has been lifted and the true consciousness of a people has been revealed. True colors and thoughts have been expressed and that genie, my friends, cannot be put back into the bottle. You have stated with a resounding roar that people of color are not accepted as equals. What do I say to that, you are wrong. We are Americans, Black Americans, and we are equal.

Figure 11 And still we wait.

Usher in November 2016 when the grand pretense was revealed with the loudest message ever. The year did not end as predicted. Every poll, commentator, and study indicated that the election would swing one way. There were a few who predicted the swing would go in the other direction. At the end of the cycle, the only question was, how could someone with no knowledge of the workings of government, no diplomacy, and a bully mentality rise to the most powerful position in the world? How could someone who never articulated a clear policy, stance, or solution, but offered insults and threats ascend to the most powerful position in the country? How could someone who advocated hate, division, and violence possibly win the most coveted position in America? How you ask; the answer is **IGNORANCE** (a lack of knowledge, learning, information), **APATHY** (lack of interest, enthusiasm, or concern), **lack of INTELLIGENCE** (lack of sound thought or good judgement), and **STUPIDITY** (behavior that shows a lack of good sense or judgement). I am sorry if this comes off as harsh, but it escapes me how someone with no qualifications for the job earns the job except for the awakening of a dormant resentment rising to the surface after the last president was a person of color. Elements of America were determined to send a message. Message received.

Figure 12 Where is America headed?

The 2016 election tapped into some realities that had been, again, lying dormant for many years. The 45th President preyed on those realities; he tapped into the suppressed emotions of the IGNORANT and exploited them. The 45th President termed his actions as "being non-politically correct"; he dressed bigotry up and said that he was just stating things as they were and "not sugar coating them". He took the country that is America and turned it against everything that it fights for every day – Democracy, a system of government by the PEOPLE.

Americans sometimes forget that the land and the people that are America have many battle wounds and scars (physical and mental) that they obtained together, side-by-side. That they have fought and struggled for years to reach a peaceful co-existence. That every day is a fight between themselves and outsiders. And that the first word in the official title of the country is "United". It took one man one year to destroy what had taken hundreds of years to build. He took the country back decades before Civil Rights, before Rights to Vote, before Roe vs Wade, before the Vietnam War, and before hundreds of Equal Opportunity, Sexual Harassment, and any other decency policies that mandated that "Americans" be civil to one another and treat one another with respect. He took a country that was trying to adhere to the adage "United we stand, divided we fall" and returned it to a more divisive country that believes it is okay to discard filters and replace those filters with what the President sugar coated as "candid speak". The 45th President liked to believe that he was being a strong, dominant, effective leader when he spewed harsh and divisive rhetoric but he was being the exact opposite of each of those.

Figure 13 United we stand, divided we fall.

I have no stake in anyone being Republican, Democrat, Independent, or Progressive. But I do have a stake in whomever is elected will be for ALL the people and not given a platform for racist bias. America cannot be this country. Americans cannot be complicit in the erosion of the country's values, what it stands for, what it was built on. Party affiliation was not on the line, it was not about a party, it was about a person. When votes are cast, hopefully those votes are based on electing the person who will aid each individual in ascending to their goal and dreams. But when we vote for hatred, no one wins. Future hopes must be placed with someone who offers some semblance of knowledge, awareness, experience, or SANITY of the issues facing the nation and not hatred and bigotry.

Figure 14 Is this the state of our country? Hatred and bigotry leads to division and internal wars.

Figure 15 Americans are a diverse group who stand by one another and live by a set of values.

The 45th President offered nothing in the way of substance on the issues to the people. He bullied, threatened, and yelled his way to the highest position in the land. He had offered nothing, but nasty remarks and he had dragged the American political system into a gutter and made American Democracy a joke and a travesty.

"We will have to repent in this generation not merely for the vitriolic words and actions of the bad people but for the appalling silence of the good people. We must come to see that human progress never rolls in on wheels of inevitability," on April 16, 1963, in the "Letter from Birmingham Jail," King carried books as he headed toward the airplane that was to take him from Atlanta to Birmingham on Oct. 30, 1967, where he faced a five-day jail sentence for parading against court orders during 1963 civil rights demonstrations in Alabama.

Figure 16 We must all get out and demand substance from our leaders.

The 45th President did not respect the PEOPLE of the country, none of the people.

"I say to you today, my friends, that in spite of the difficulties and frustrations of the moment, I still have a dream," these are the words of Martin Luther King, Jr. on August 28, 1963, from his "I Have a Dream" speech.

As 2020 rang in, it brought hope, new possibilities, and enthusiasm. But it was shortly thereafter that the world would begin speaking of some new mystery virus that was ravishing Wuhan, China, it was a novel coronavirus. A virus that would eventually ravish or consume the world. A virus that would change the way the world lived and day-to-day lives. A virus that would change how the world interacted with one another. It would be asked, what was this new and dangerous virus? But a bigger and more important question would become, how would America handle the crisis that would affect more than two million people and cause the death of more than one hundred and twenty-five thousand?

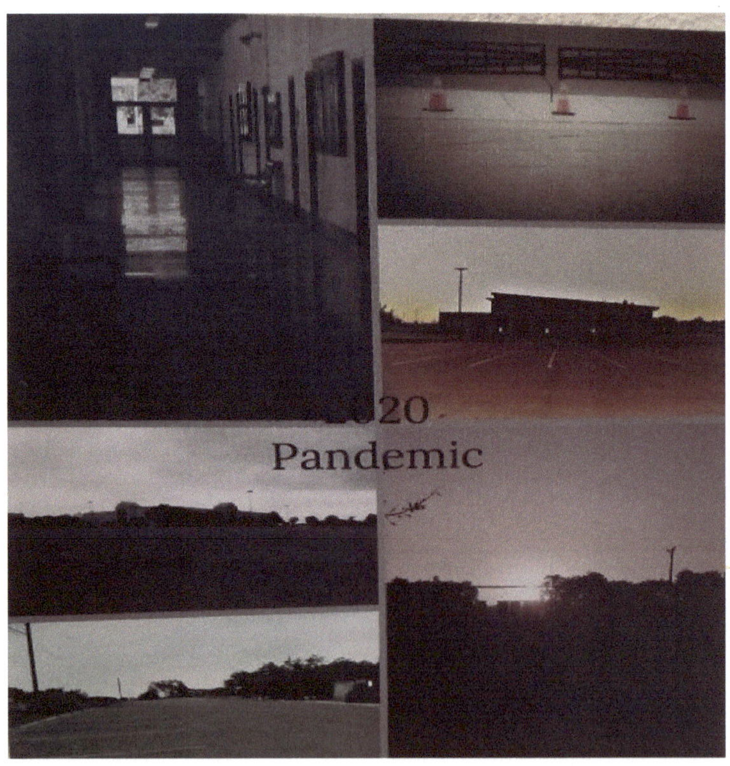

Figure 17 The crisis that revealed cracks in the armor of the country's leadership.

The concern medical experts had regarding the mystery virus soon turned to alarm. It would be a month after word of the mysterious virus before America would take action to contain the outbreak. At that point, officials had effectively concluded that America had already lost the fight to contain the virus and that the country needed to switch to mitigation. As the virus cases mounted the President rallied for his own campaign and dismissed what was fast becoming a horrible reality. By the time America was forced to acknowledge that a deadly virus was in their backyard, and it had to deal with it, the country had lost its first citizen to the virus. But for two months, the inaction of the President left an opening for 2 million travelers to travel into the country, without restrictions, from all over the world and many would be host to the virus.

The status quo was crumbling, there was no guidance from the federal government, the states and municipalities were on their own. Governors shut down their states to try and stop the spread. By April 2020, the US cases had even surpassed China, the country of origin of the virus. And by Memorial Day 2020, COVID-19 had claimed more US lives than the Vietnam (1964, 58,220), Gulf (1991, 2,586), Afghanistan (2001, 2,349), and Iraq (2003, 4,418) Wars combined (97,000+).

Figure 18 Remembering those lost.

A nation, built on forward motion, was told that the only way to get through the crisis was to SHUTDOWN/STOP/STAY HOME. So, in March of 2020, the hospitals geared up for the 200,000 people that would be rushed in, 124,000 schools would shut down, and 38 million people suddenly had no paycheck. It was during this time that the country's great divide was again revealed, the disparities in wealth. The crisis revealed that 55% of Americans got to stay home, had jobs, and received their salaries, but the lowest paid workers (a large percentage, people of color) did not have that luxury, they could not stay home; they had to show up to work putting themselves and their families at risk daily. And because this segment of the population was out confronting the virus every day, a disproportionate number of them were contracting the virus and dying at a larger rate.

So, with 38 million people out of work, more than 13% unemployment, more than 2 million Americans affected with the virus, and more than 125 thousand American deaths from the virus, the President determined that the country would reopen despite the continued rise in numbers in all areas. Looking ahead to re-election, the 45th President saw a tanking economy as a complete roadblock to his reelection. With that at the forefront of his mind, things such as loss of American lives (lives of color) and fears of returning to normalcy because the virus is not contained, the President said "we need to get the economy back, people want to go back to work." And so, the country began to reopen despite lack of containment.

Figure 19 Economic and health crisis collide.

The year had already dealt the blow of two crises, health and economic, and then the American people would have to deal with yet another crisis, a third crisis, atrocities committed against Black Americans. As the virus cases continued to mount, there was also a rise in protesting. The protest stemmed from another senseless death of a Black American by a White police officer. The police officer was caught on video with his knee on the neck of George Floyd and he held his knee on his neck for nearly 9 minutes (8 minutes and 46 seconds). It was heart wrenching and agonizing to watch. Two minutes and 53 seconds of this time George Floyd was non-responsive. This clear disregard for life lit a spark of anger in the communities around the country and the world. But then the question came, how would the President handle this third crisis, and the answer, with hatred, bigotry, and denial. The images from the video were gut wrenching and were destined to invoke anger, contempt, and a desire to want to strike back. The senseless killings of Black Americans had to stop and the only way to make those killings stop was to hold those responsible for the deaths, who showed a clear disregard for humanity, accountable for their actions. The President's inability to even acknowledge racism's existence and particularly his role in perpetuating the hatred and bigotry led many to believe there would be no help coming from the highest office. Racism disguised as serve and protect should not be protected by antiquated laws and should not lead to automatic freedom from prosecution when the actions and intentions are reprehensible and clear. Justice should be immediate and swift as it would be with anyone else that committed a crime of that nature. But American history has not supported this, and so the atrocities against people of color continue.

Figure 20 American people, black, brown, white, all.

"We must either learn to live together as brothers or we are all going to perish together as fools," Martin Luther King, Jr., December 24, 1967, a Christmas sermon. As the turmoil of three crises (health, economic, and social) continued in 2020, leadership was hard pressed to address any of them head on. America's flaws were on full display, particularly racism. The cracks in the American armor were becoming painfully clear.

It was becoming clear that another question had to be posed, what was really causing the problems that Americans were observing? It was becoming clear that Americans would have to go back to the beginning when immigrants from all over traveled to a land in hopes of a new and safe beginning. There was no White or Black, it was a coalition of Others. But somehow as time went on it simply became White vs Black. Everyone must acknowledge the advantages White Americans have been given over others for no other reason than the color of their skin. Not because they were smarter or better, just because they were White, and they received all the early advantages. The first step in combating this disparity in treatment, and maybe the hardest step, is to first acknowledge it, acknowledge that the system is not always fair. Racism is a powerful institution, and it exists, built by 400 years of slavery, 150 years of discrimination (overt), and another 50 years of covert discrimination. A legacy this long in the making does not just disappear overnight, Americans are going to have to actively work at it.

Figure 21 Let this legacy set.

"We are no longer going to allow you to pretend that we are somehow subhuman, we are not interested in conditional freedom we want the freedom that we damn well deserve and we want it right now."

Jesse Williams
Actor/Activist
2016 BET Awards

"BLACK LIVES MATTER" is not a hate group it's simply a group of tired individuals who are fighting for equality and justice."

Centric
The first network designed for Black women.

"It's about getting the narrative straight, and the narrative is we are not a movement about harming police, we are a movement about holding police accountable."

Stay Woke
Black Lives Matter Movement

Figure 22 Out of the shadow. Grant me full access.

Yes, all lives matter, absolutely, but it is not all lives being taken in the streets of America, it is Black lives. The senseless killings of Black Americans has to end.

It has been stated that if you can survive being Black in America, you can survive anything. The protesters that took to the streets in 2020 wanted one simple thing and that was to end the violence and killings against Black Americans. They wanted reforms of how law enforcement was conducted, and they wanted to eliminate the legal protections that police officers received despite the unjust killings they may be a part of. Let the justice system judge their actions. Black Americans have suffered, suffered 400 years after slavery, decades after the Civil Rights Act, and years after police shot and killed Michael Brown in Ferguson. And still in 2020, Blacks were more likely to be killed by police because of the adversarial nature of their relationship. They were also dying at an alarming rate of COVID-19, a much higher rate than White Americans. And Blacks were more likely to have lost their jobs in the economic crisis.

Keep the anger, continue to peacefully protest, and continue to demand an inalienable right that ALL Americans have been given. On March 31, 1968, Martin Luther King Jr. said, *"…without this hard work, time itself becomes an ally of the primitive forces of social stagnation. So we must help time and realize that the time is always ripe to do right."* King said this during his "Remaining Awake Through a Great Revolution" sermon at the National Cathedral in Washington D.C. Four days later he was assassinated.

Figure 23 This is what we are years after slavery and civil rights. We are brothers and sisters.

Langston Hughes – 1902-1967

A poet, novelist, fiction writer, and playwright, Langston Hughes is known for his insightful, colorful portrayals of black life in America from the twenties through the sixties and was important in shaping the artistic contributions of the Harlem Renaissance.

I, too, sing America.

I am the darker brother.
They send me to eat in the kitchen
When company comes,
But I laugh,
And eat well,
And grow strong.

Tomorrow,
I'll be at the table
When company comes.
Nobody'll dare
Say to me,
"Eat in the kitchen,"
Then.

Besides,
They'll see how beautiful I am
And be ashamed—

I, too, am America.

"I, **Too**" is a poem written by **Langston Hughes** that demonstrates a yearning for equality through perseverance while disproving the idea that patriotism is limited by race. It was first published in 1926 and published in The Weary Blues.

At a crossroad, as Americans bear witness to the racial strife that is gripping the country, they have to ask themselves another question, how do we get past the feeling that Black Americans have been deceived by the promise of America? With all the advances of Black Americans, they can still feel tired and hopeless and doubt their own accomplishments. But it is because of their forward motion, no matter how slow or slight, that they should maintain hope. Despite an onslaught of movements, setbacks, and disappointments, Black Americans continue to prevail.

Black Americans are a resilient people. We continue to rise as we resist hate. We continue to believe that if there is good in people that the promise of America will be granted to all. We continue to remember the words that our parents continuously expressed to us, that they wanted more for us than they had for themselves. We continue to strive for that American dream. We also remember that with every push our parents gave us to strive for that dream that it always came with a cautionary attachment, that the path would not be an easy one.

Figure 24 Beacon of hope.

With each small victory, Black Americans, should bask in that victory if only for a moment and then confront the next hurdle. People of color are also told that they must work twice as hard as their White counterparts to achieve any modicum of the dream. This is work that has to be put in, after all it is what Black Americans do, and it is what they have always had to do. The battle cry of Black America is to never give up. It is through the struggles that change comes. And even if those changes seem small, they may be transformational. And so, the message is always, never give up and never stop hoping.

Figure 25 The promise.

"If you can be black and live in this world you can be anything you want to be," Cicely Tyson, BET Black Girls Rock 2015. We America, are at a cross in the road. George Floyd's killing opened a wound that has never really healed. That wound is the ugly truth that Black American's opportunities are hard fought, and that discrimination exist for them. People of color are not afforded true inalienable rights of "Life, Liberty, and the pursuit of Happiness," promised to all Americans in the Declaration of Independence that states that "all men are created equal."   The promise of July 4, 1776, has not been a reality for all Americans. Abraham Lincoln said during the Civil War that, *"A house divided against itself cannot stand."* Why are differences so divisive? It must be remembered that we are *all* Americans-white, black, or brown, native-born or recent immigrated citizen; that it is the diversity that makes America America. Americans cannot solely look to the leaders to make change; genuine change must come from individuals. Americans must delve into their hearts and minds and work within the communities and cities to make genuine and lasting change. To get America back on course toward the promise of the better life to which we all aspire, back on track to providing equal opportunity for everyone, and back to a renewed commitment of the American dream, we must work as a unified America.

Figure 26 United States of America.

SAY THEIR NAME

TRAYVON MARTIN February 2012, age 17

ERIC GARNER July 2014, age 43

MICHAEL BROWN August 2014, age 18

TAMIR RICE November 2014, age 12

BREONNA TAYLOR March 2020, age 26

GEORGE FLOYD May 2020, age 46

Rayshard Brooks June 2020, age 27

These names made it to national news but how many did not? Let's renew our commitment to the American dream for us all.

THE DREAM

The American dream is the same for us all.

Will America let the sun set on my dream?